1 - 10 - 2017

For: Sam & Donna

Love,
Mary Derrick :♡

Someone To Watch Over Me

Additional copies may be ordered from the publisher for educational, business, promotional or premium use. For information, contact ALIVE Book Publishing at: alivebookpublishing.com or call (925) 837-7303.

Book Design by Alex Johnson

ISBN 13
978-1-63132-036-1

ISBN 10
1-63132-036-X

Library of Congress Control Number: 2016953543
Library of Congress Cataloging-in-Publication Data is available upon request.

First Edition

Published in the United States of America
by ALIVE Book Publishing and ALIVE Publishing Group,
imprints of Advanced Publishing LLC
3200 A Danville Blvd., Suite 204, Alamo, California 94507
alivebookpublishing.com

PRINTED IN THE UNITED STATES OF AMERICA

10 9 8 7 6 5 4 3 2 1

Someone To Watch Over Me

by

Lucy Grace Yaldezian

Artwork by Mary Derrick

ABOOKS
Alive Book Publishing

My Grateful Thanks To

Chris George Yaldezian
for keeping the faith all these years.

Alexander Gary Palangian for inspiring this concept.

Vimala Rodgers for the beautiful gift of this soul-based system of writing
& permission to use her copyrighted material in this book.

Mary Derrick for her heart-centered artwork and generous spirit.

All those whose support and encouragement infused these pages.

Foreword

This small book is far more than that; it is a treasure. From Lucy Grace's familiarity with the spiritual essence of each of the 26 Letters, she introduces each of them as "who they are," along with the precious 26 Guardian Protectors, each of whom lives within a specific Letter. They come alive as true and trusted friends, experts in guiding the reader to a solution that comes from the noblest part of themselves.

Through practical life experiences, the reader is invited to call upon both the Letter and the Guardian Protector of that Letter, in order to get to know them as dear trusted friends who always understand, never judge, and are guided to help the reader "out of a pickle," as it were—like receiving advice from someone who knows everything about you, and loves you anyway—without hesitation. The Guardian Protector of that Letter then asks a question relevant to the meaning of the Letter at hand. By engaging in a dialog, readers both young and not-so-young are able to awaken the soul-energy within themselves that makes them feel good about themselves from the inside out.

Although Lucy Grace wrote this book with children in mind, I'm buying it for many adults I know—and am keeping a copy next to my bed.

Dr. Vimala Rodgers,
Rancho Cordova, CA

A Note to the Adult Reading This Book

Whether your spiritual beliefs include the structure of a specific faith or not, this book offers a door to making the intangibility of faith accessible and real to a child, an avenue of spiritual comfort, protection and guidance. I wrote this book to create a shared experience between an adult and cherished child.

The Vimala Alphabet
&
Guardian Protectors

Dr. Vimala Rodgers has made a life-long study of the letters of the alphabet. Her orientation includes ancient traditions of letters as Sacred Symbols.

The cursive-based font you see throughout the book is based on The Vimala System of Handwriting. Each letter formation in the Vimala Alphabet is specific and purposeful. This is not just a way to transfer thoughts to paper via a pen. The Vimala System of Handwriting is a comprehensive character-building process. Children taught to write according to The Vimala System grow up to be dynamic, critical thinkers and responsible, curious, kind, confident individuals. Adults who adopt The Vimala Alphabet notice self-sabotaging patterns, behaviors and beliefs falling away as self-affirming ones root.

I adopted The Vimala Alphabet in 1994 and can attest to its transformative results. It is an extraordinary avenue for personal excellence at any age.

This little book is based on each letter in The Vimala Alphabet having its own "Guardian Protector."

Pay special attention to the pages covering the first letter of the child's first and last names, at birth, for they are particularly meaningful.

There is room on each page for the child to draw a picture of the Guardian Protector of that particular letter. When drawing the picture, encourage him/her to sketch it out first with his/her left hand and then color it in with the right. Especially for a right-handed child, the left hand is a gateway to magical areas of the brain that he/she may not normally get to use. What fun! The more any of us writes and draws with the non-dominant hand, the better the brain will work as a whole. Yes, this can make us all smarter and more creative!

The Vimala Alphabet, declarations and individual Guardian Protectors are solely based on the work of Vimala Rodgers of The International Institute of Handwriting Studies (IIHS), and used here by permission. All other content is my own.

Dearest Little One,

This book introduces you to some very unusual beings. Most of them are Angels and some of them are Heavenly Guides.

Angels are hard to describe. They look sort of human, but they are in a category all their own. They can talk to us without words. Some of them have huge white wings and can fly like birds. Others look just like regular people but they have a very sweet manner and a very bright light that comes from them.

Heavenly Guides don't have wings but they surely do have special powers and lots of wisdom to help us. Angels and Heavenly Guides are wondrous creatures whose job it is to do God's work on Earth. What is God? Think of a loving goodness that is the greatest force and power in the Universe, and that begins to describe God.

Did you know that every person who has ever lived or ever will live has a part of them that lasts forever? This is your soul or spirit. Your spirit makes you uniquely you. If you ever forget that, just look at your fingertips. See the tiny marks there? These are your fingerprints and they are one-of-a-kind. That's right. No one who has ever lived before you or will ever live after you has the same fingerprints as you. This is God's guarantee that you are special and very important.

So is it any wonder that God gives us heavenly Guides and Angels to help us whenever we need it? These Guides and Angels are messengers, protectors, nurturers and bridges between the spiritual world and our human world.

Some people call that spiritual world "heaven." I think of it as a place of pure light, filled with nothing but love. I believe that we all come from that spiritual world and return to it when we die. Each of the Angels and Heavenly Guides in these pages is available to you – to any of us – at any time. If you're curious about the connection to the letters of the alphabet, read the next section.

Develop a friendship with each of the Angels and Heavenly Guides introduced here. There's space for you to draw a picture of each one. You can get to know them better by thinking of them, talking to them when you have quiet moments alone, listening for them, and watching for their messages. These messages tend to show up in creative ways such as in the words of a song that you hear on the radio, or the words or picture on a billboard you pass on the road, or a sign on a truck driving by. Those messages can also come in the form of a sweet, gentle voice in your head or a warm feeling in your heart. Your Angels and Heavenly Guides are never critical or mean. Their purpose and path is loving service to us human beings.

Have fun getting to know them all. They are always, always available to help you. They love you even more than your Mommy or Daddy or grandparents or aunts or uncles do – and you know that's a lot!

With love from *Lucy Grace*

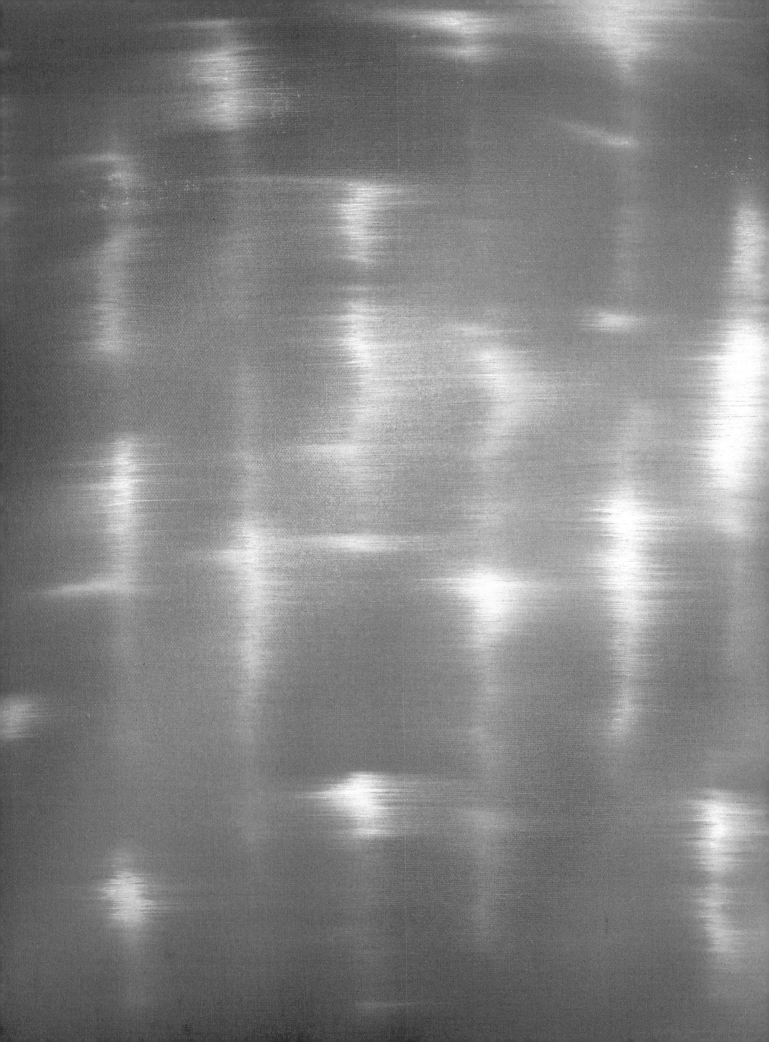

Aa *The light inside me brightens the whole world.*

Gabriel (Gahb-ree-el') is the Angel of Rebirth. Every morning begins a brand new day. Within each day there are countless opportunities to open our minds in new ways, change patterns for the better, make important corrections in behavior or actions or thoughts.

When you think about it, every moment is a new beginning. Call upon hopeful Gabriel whenever you want help making a new start of any kind.

What examples of new beginnings can you think of?

Gabriel

Bb   *I like To have everyone win.*

Zadkiel (Zahd'-kee-el) is the Angel of Prayer. Prayer is talking to God and there are many ways to pray. You can put your hands together, close your eyes and bow your head to pray silently or softly. You might also enjoy dancing or singing your prayers.

Saying "thank you" for all the good things and people in your life is a wonderful prayer. Zadkiel can help you find the best way to pray in any situation.

What's your favorite way to pray?

Zadkiel

Cc

I know that I am taken care of.

Quan Yin (Kwan Yin) is a Heavenly Guide. She is the one who "looks at the world with the eyes of compassion." "Compassion" means caring about other people and their feelings.

If you're having trouble forgiving a friend who hurt you or made you mad, beautiful Quan Yin can help. Whenever your heart feels like a closed fist inside your chest, call on kind, understanding Quan Yin to help you trust again.

What makes your heart happy to think about?

Quan Yin

Dd

I am respectful of others.

Ongkannon (Ahn'-ka-non) is the Angel of Communication. *Communication* is a long word that means connecting with others. There are many ways to communicate but one of the most common is by talking.

Have you noticed that everyone has an opinion, everyone has a point of view? Sometimes that opinion is the same as yours, sometimes it's different. The differences may be tiny or so great that it's hard to even find a way to talk to each other. If you're ever in that situation, call on Ongkannon because she has a way of pointing out the common ground.

What's your favorite subject to talk to a friend about?

Ongkannon

$\mathcal{E}$ εe _I enjoy being with people who are different from me._

Kaelarae (Kai-lah'-rai) is the Angel of Peace. Sometimes the world can be too full: too much to do, too many thoughts in your head, too much clutter, too much noise. When you notice that happening, Kaelarae is the one who can guide you to a peaceful, quiet, restful place deep down inside of your very own self.

Imagine a land of peace behind your belly button you could travel to anytime, simply by thinking about it. Kaelarae knows just where it is.

What would that peaceful place look like, smell like, feel like?

Kaelarae

F f

*My imagination helps me
do great things.*

Jophiel (Jo-fee-el') is the Angel of Creative Power. Jophiel knows that you have a way of drawing or singing or dancing or making up stories that's like nobody else. Jophiel is a master at helping you to create something brand new, something that never existed before.

Remember that whatever you create doesn't have to be perfect. Have fun!

What's your favorite way to use your imagination?

Jophiel

Gg   _I am so happy to be who I am._

Ooniemme (Oh-nee-em') is the Angel of Gratitude. Gratitude means being thankful. At least once a day, think about three or more things, people, happenings that you're grateful for. Holding Ooniemme's hand when you do this makes it extra-special.

If you ever can't think of anything to be grateful for, call upon Ooniemme to whisper good suggestions in your ear.

What are you most grateful for today?

Ooniemme

Hh   *I am courageous!*

Cerviel (Sir-vee-el') is the Angel of Courage. Whenever you need to face a hard task or situation, Cerviel is the perfect friend to call upon. She will remind you that you are both brave and strong, and will help you be even braver and stronger whenever you need to be.

Think about how your body feels when you're feeling scared. Now think about how your body feels when you're feeling brave.

What's your body's favorite feeling?

Cerviel

Ii   *I pay attention.*

Shekinah (Shek-ee'-nah) is the Angel of Unity. Does it ever feel like your thoughts and your actions are pulling you in different directions? Shekinah brings your thoughts and actions together in a way that helps you be your best.

When you are having trouble seeing a situation clearly, Shekinah can help you sharpen your focus.

What would it be like to have Shekinah sit by you in school all day?

Shekinah

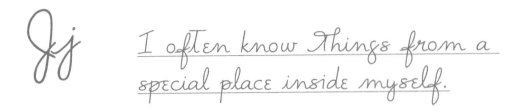

I often know things from a special place inside myself.

Rafael (Rah-fah-el') is the Angel of Inner Healing. There's a special light in each and every one of us. Sometimes that light is bright and really easy to see; sometimes it gets dim. No matter how dim it may get, that light never completely shuts off. Even after we die, that special light burns on.

Rafael is a master at helping you keep your inner light shiny and bright, no matter how dark and dull you may feel.

What color is that special light inside of you?

Rafael

Kk

I know when I need to listen and when I need to speak.

Galgaliel (Gal-gal'-ee-el) is the Angel of Good Energy. Have you noticed how one grumpy kid can pull everyone else in the room down? The opposite happens, too. One really happy kid in a group can help brighten everyone up.

Galgaliel is the Angel who can fix bad energy in people and situations as easily as a clever handyman can fix something broken in the house.

What are some nice things you can say, or do, to make the world a happier place?

Galgaliel

Ll *I keep my inner light bright, strong and clear.*

Nisroc (Niz'-rok) is the Angel of Freedom. Have you ever watched a hawk flying? Hawks and eagles and other large birds know how to find special waves of air called thermals that carry them in the sky. Imagine what it would be like to ride the thermals like a bird. What freedom!

When Nisroc takes your hand, wherever you are, whatever else is going on, you can feel as light and free as a bird flying high in the sky. The best freedom is when your inner light is bright and clear and strong.

Where would you go if you could fly?

Nisroc

Mm   _I enjoy being with other people._

Ananchel (Ah'-nan-kel) is the Angel of Divine Grace. Have you ever seen beams of golden sunlight shining out through a hole in dark rainclouds? That's Divine Grace. It's God's promise that everything's okay, no matter what. Ananchel is a special messenger of God's light. The more you call upon Ananchel, the better you will understand what Divine Grace is all about.

Ask Ananchel to surround you with God's light every day, even before you get out of bed. Imagine your best friend walking around in a bubble of light. Imagine the members of your family and your friends each walking around in a bubble of light. That thought puts a huge smile on Ananchel's face. Close your eyes and see Ananchel smiling at you.

How might the world be different if every human and animal were surrounded by God's light?

Ananchel

Nn   <u>I have good friends</u>
              <u>who can count on me.</u>

Ramaela (Rah-my'-lah) is the Angel of Playfulness. Are those
sneakers peeking out from under Ramaela's white angel robe?
Of course! Ramaela is always ready for fun and adventure.
When you're having fun with a good friend, you can be sure Ramaela is there with you. When you're being a kind and thought-
ful friend, Ramaela's smile is wider than the sky.

If you ever feel gloomy, call on Ramaela. In no time the two of
you will be jumping around like a couple of chimpanzees, laugh-
ing until your sides hurt!

What activities do you like to share with friends?

Ramaela

O o _My words are kind and helpful._

Amitiel (Ah-mee'-tee-el) is the Angel of Truth. Amitiel reminds us that we can be truthful without being hurtful. It's important to tell the truth, and it's important to be kind. Whenever you need help saying what you mean honestly and kindly, ask Amitiel for the right words.

Amitiel knows that words become golden when they pass through your heart before coming out of your mouth.

Who would appreciate some kind words from you?

Amitiel

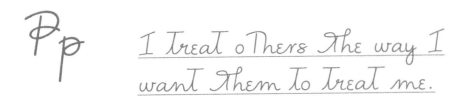

Pp   <u>I Treat others the way I want them to treat me.</u>

Charmiene (Shar-mee-en') is the Angel of Harmony. What happens when you play any two notes together on a musical instrument? Some combinations of notes are downright ugly, making you squirm and wince; others are so pleasant, you want to hear more. When two or more notes create a beautiful sound, that's harmony.

Charmiene loves to focus on your harmony with yourself. We all do dumb things sometimes or get mad at ourselves for this or that. When you're in that spot, Charmiene will flutter her wings ever so slightly around you. This is her way of reminding you what a good person you are and how deeply you are loved by God, Mom, Dad, grandmas, grandpas, aunties, uncles, cousins, friends … boy, that's a lot of love for you!

What makes you feel loved?

Charmiene

Qq   *I enjoy helping others.*

Uriel (You-ree-el') is the Angel of Selfless Service. The good feeling you get inside your heart when you do something kind or generous for someone else – maybe someone you don't even know – that's Uriel's reward for you.

Some people ignore Uriel's gentle call to be of service to others and think only about themselves, their needs, their desires. How wonderful that you're not like that! When you give some of your toys away to other children so they can enjoy playing with them, Uriel is standing right next to you, beaming with pride.

Were you helpful to someone today?

Uriel

Rrr *I love to use my imagination.*

Rohana (Ro-hah'-nah) is the Angel of Applied Creativity and is a great friend of Jophiel. Sometimes they hang out together. If you need to make a volcano for a science fair project, call upon Rohana. She'll whisper in your ear ideas to make it uniquely yours, unlike any other student's volcano.

Imagine taking a book you've read and turning into a play – that's the kind of thing Rohana loves to do.

What favorite story or book can you act out to make a play?

Rohana

Ss _I can be calm when I need To._

Ariel (Ar-ee-el') is the Angel of Nature. TV shows, movies, videogames are all fun, but there's nothing like being out in nature. A visit to a park or a short walk around the neighborhood – our beautiful planet always has gifts to share if we take the time to look. No one knows the power of nature better than Ariel. This quiet Angel has a sweet smile and peaceful eyes.

When you're feeling confused or upset, call upon Ariel, and she'll wrap you in the quiet strength of the mountains, the reliable calm of the ocean, the purpose of each season. Ariel knows that no matter how crazy life gets, nature offers balance and order.

Where do you like to go to be in nature?

Ariel

TTЯ
I am making The world
a happier place.

Paschar (Poo-shar') is the Angel of Vision, and you'll be glad to know her. When you're working on a project and start feeling like you want to give up, Paschar can be there in an instant to cheer you to the finish.

Paschar is a powerhouse when it comes to giving you the discipline and enthusiasm you need to reach any goal you set for yourself, big or little. Yay Paschar, yay you!

What goal would you like to reach?

Paschar

Uu   _I listen carefully when I_
      am learning something new.

Metatron (Met'-a-tron) is the Angel of Thought. Metatron, and his twin brother, Sandalphon (see the Letter Xx), are gi-nor-mous —larger than Planet Earth! Having an open mind is so important that one of the most powerful Angels was put in charge of that.

You know that expression "Garbage in, garbage out"? Well, it's not just about what you put into a computer. It goes for the thoughts and ideas that you put into your mind as well. Meta-tron will help you respect your mind and thoughts.

How do you keep your mind open and shiny?

Metatron

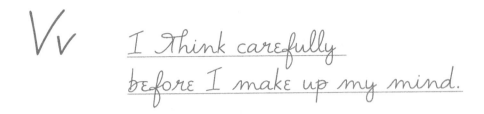

Vv

I think carefully before I make up my mind.

Zagzagel (Zagh'-zagh-el) is the Angel of Wisdom. Sometimes decisions are easy to make, and sometimes they're hard. The worry of making the wrong decision can be the hardest part.

The next time you need to make a tough decision, call upon Zagzagel. He'll make sure that you sift through all the options and come up with the best answer.

What tough decisions have you had to make?

Zazzagel

Ww   *I love to share what I have learned.*

Jesus Christ (Gee'-zus Kryst) is a Heavenly Guide who teaches many important messages from God about love. He shared those messages through stories so we could understand them easily and live them better.

What you share with love creates goodness and more love. The more you get to know Jesus Christ, the more you learn about how love can make the world a better place.

How do you share what's important to you?

Jesus Christ

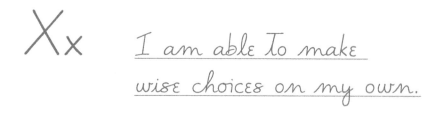

Xx   *I am able to make
wise choices on my own.*

Sandalphon (Sand'-al-fon) is the Angel of Power. Remember
Metatron? This is his equally tall twin brother, bigger than Planet
Earth! He's not someone to mess with. Call upon Sandalphon
whenever you need to be reminded to stand tall and have faith in
yourself.

If someone tries to convince you to do something you know is
wrong, it's hard sometimes not to give in. In a situation like that,
Sandalphon will help you stay strong and do what you know is
right. What a great feeling that is!

How can you tell the difference between doing something that's
right, and doing something that's wrong?

Sandalphon

Yy   *My ideas are important.*

Sarasvati (Sahr-ahs'-vhat-ee) is the Heavenly Guide of Music, Knowledge and the Arts. Even her name is pretty to say and hear. Music, learning, drawing, painting, dancing, acting – how dull the world would be without them!

Whether you're appreciating the music or playing or singing it, admiring the painting or creating it with your brush, Sarasvati will inspire, encourage and applaud you. Take a bow!

Have you ever been to a museum, or sung in a concert, or acted in a play?

Sarasvati

33 _I love my life!_

Zacharael (Zah-kah-ry-el') is the Angel of Surrender. You may think of "surrender" as giving up, and sometimes that's a bad thing; but Zacharael's focus is the surrender that allows us to trust that something good comes out of everything. Everything. Even something that may seem bad while it's happening has a gift in it somewhere, somehow. Call upon Zacharael whenever you need help finding that trust, that gift.

Remember: All is moving toward the good ... and so it is.

What's your favorite way of remembering that life is good?

Zacharael

For more information about The Vimala Alphabet and System of Handwriting, including the Soul Quality of each letter, the books of Dr. Vimala Rodgers are invaluable: *Change Your Handwriting, Change Your Life; Your Handwriting Can Change Your Life; and Transform Your Life Through Handwriting.* Also visit www.iihs.com.

About the Author

Lucy Grace Yaldezian established A Higher Perspective, a successful healing arts practice, in 1992. Her mind-body-spirit toolbox for adults, teens, and children includes hypnotherapy, The Emotional Freedom Technique (EFT), The Tapas Acupressure Technique (TAT), and, of course, the Vimala System of Handwriting.

lucy@ahigherperspective.com
www.ahigherperspective.com

About the Illustrator

Mary E. Lavin-Derrick, LMP began painting and soon realized she was an intuitive artist. This skill led to the healing of her inner-child. Others have received similar results by taking her art workshop called *Playing with Color*. She lives in the little village of Fall City, WA, just below beautiful Snoqualmie Falls…a magical place.

ABOOKS

ALIVE Book Publishing and ALIVE Publishing Group
are imprints of Advanced Publishing LLC,
3200 A Danville Blvd., Suite 204, Alamo, California 94507

Telephone: 925.837.7303 Fax: 925.837.6951
www.alivebookpublishing.com

CPSIA information can be obtained
at www.ICGtesting.com
Printed in the USA
BVOW10*0829020117

472332BV00022BA/284/P